Words from my Mentor Dr L.V Mangue.
FART ON THE BULLY, NO BULLY CAN
BULLY YOU. TELL THE BULLY TO BE A
BUDDY NOT A BULLY.

My Characters will speak out loud.
Setting an example for all Gifted
Children future. BE A BUDDY NOT A BULLY.

AuthorHouse™
1663 Liberty Drive
Bloomington, IN 47403
www.authorhouse.com
Phone: 833-262-8899

Because of the dynamic nature of the Internet, any web addresses or links contained in this book may have changed
since publication and may no longer be valid. The views expressed in this work are solely those of the author and do
not necessarily reflect the views of the publisher, and the publisher hereby disclaims any responsibility for them.

Any people depicted in stock imagery provided by Getty Images are models,
and such images are being used for illustrative purposes only.
Certain stock imagery © Getty Images.

This book is printed on acid-free paper.

ISBN: 978-1-6655-5400-8 (sc)
ISBN: 978-1-6655-5401-5 (e)

Print information available on the last page.

Published by AuthorHouse 03/15/2022

authorHOUSE®

1

CHAPTER

✦ ✦ ✦ ✦ ✦

COVID-19 HAS OPEN DOORS FOR EVERYONE
IT HAS LEFT A BAD TASTE IN OUR MOUTHS
WHAT HAS MANKIND DONE THAT WAS SO WRONG
TO BROUGHT DOWN WRATH ON ALL JESUS CHILDREN
WHAT'S IS THE INVISIBLE ACT THAT'S TAKEN PLACE
BEHIND CLOSE DOORS AND IN PLAIN SIGHT.

THE WORLD HAS BEEN FACED WITH CRISIS THAT THEY
WASN'T PREPARED FOR, WEARING A MASK WAS NOT ON
ANYONE'S AGENDA. AMERICA HAS TO GEAR UP TO TREAT
INVISIBLE VIRUS FROM THE MIDDLE OF NOWHERE, WHY
POINT FINGERS AND BLAME IT ON CHINA. LETS DIG DEEP
TO FIND THE ANSWER THAT EVERYONE HAS GIVEN A BLIND
EYE TO, OVER THE YEARS. BULLYING SAGA.

WHO ARE THE BULLIES IN THE WORKPLACE,
HOSPITALS, NURSING HOMES, ASSISTED LIVING
AND EVEN CHURCHES. THIS'S A QUESTION THAT
NEEDS TO BE ANSWERED OPENLY. THIS WORLD IS
SO CORRUPT THAT TARGETING A PERSON BEHIND
CLOSE DOORS WITH LIES AND FALSE DOCUMENTATION
WILL COME TO LIGHT SOMEDAY.

BULLIES ARE EVERYWHERE, THEY'RE USUALLY THE
ONES WITH THE LOUDEST MOUTHS. THEY HAVE
ABUNDANCE OF SO CALLED FRIENDS TO BACK THEM
UP IN WHATEVER THE SITUATION IS. LIES ARE CRIPPLING
FAMILIES AND MOST DEFINITELY IN THE WORKING ENVIRONMENTS.
THIS CORRUPTION PLAYS A VITAL PART OF COVID-19 IT'S INVISIBLE
AND NEEDS TO BE VISIBLE FOR ALL TO READ AND TAKE NOTES.

BULLIES JUDGES, BECAUSE THAT'S WHAT THEY GET PAID TO DO.
THEY PREYS ON CO-WORKERS WEAKNESS LIKE A PIECE OF T-BONE
STEAK. THEY DIG IN, DIG IN UNTIL THEY REALIZES THAT THE STEAK IS
RAW, IT NEEDS SEASONING AND THE RIGHT TEMPERATURE TO BE OF
ANY USE TO THE GASTRIC SYSTEM. SO I ASK JESUS WHAT TO DO AGAIN
WHEN FACE WITH BULLIES IN THE WORKPLACE. TAKE A MOMENT OF SILENCE, PRAY
INTERNALLY THEN BURST A BIG FART SO LOUD,EVEN THE HUMAN RESOURCE COULD FEEL
THE TREMOR FROM THE EARTHQUAKE. LET'S MOVE ON TO THE NEXT PAGE.

2

---◆◆◆---

THIS IS THE MOMENT WE WOULD ASK OURSELVES OPENLY, WHAT
WOULD JESUS DO IF HE WAS FACE WITH VICIOUS BULLIES. WOULD HE TELL THEM TO STAY IN
THEIR LANE, OR WOULD HE STILL BE NICE TO THEM ANYWAY.
I CAN ONLY SAY, SEEING THE GOOD IN ALL PEOPLE COULD GIVE US A LEE WAY. USING OUR OPEN
MINDED KEY COULD PASS ON IN A RELAY.
WE COULD WIN FROM THE ANGLE THAT LINES UP PEACEFULLY WITH OUR FAITH, MORALS
AND DIGNITY.

BUT HOW MUCH CAN A PERSON TAKE, IN A WICKED WORLD OF PLAGUES AND LEACHES THAT'S
NEVER BACKS DOWN IN A VERY
SMALL SPACE, WHERE THE ARM LENGTH RULE IS UNDERMINED AND
OVERLOOKED, AND EVEN LOOK DOWN ON
WHERE SAFETY FIRST IS ALWAYS ON THE BACK BURNER,AND A PERSON EGO STEPS IN TO
CONTROL AND SHOWS POWER, AND
OWNERSHIP OF ONE ANOTHER FREEDOM OF SPEECH IN THE WORKPLACE.

WHERE CAN WE FIT IN, IF THERE'S NO NEED TO, HOW CAN WE
SHARE LOVE, WHEN THERE'S NO LOVE AMONG US, WHERE CAN WE
FIND PEACE IN TARNISHING ONE'S CHARACTER. CONFUSION AND MISERY ARE CONTROLLING
THIS COUNTRY, THANK GOD FOR FOREIGNERS WHO CAN SEE THROUGH THIS CHAPTER.

ALL BULLIES NEEDS TO BE DISCIPLINED, THEIR LIES NEED TO BE A TURBAN ON THEIR HEADS,
RESPECTING EACH OTHER CULTURE
IS TRUTH FROM THE BORDER. NO MORE BARRIERS AND WALLS
INVISIBLE JESUS KNOWS HOW TO CROSS OVER TO THE OTHER SIDE.
RESPECT EACH OTHER AND STOP FOCUSING ON ONE UNKNOWN STRUCTURE.

3

◆ ◆ ◆ ◆

BULLIES ARE IN EVERY CAREERS, DOCTORS, LAWYERS, NURSES
POLICEMEN, SOLDIERS, PHLEBOTOMIST,EMT'S,CAREGIVERS SUPERVISORS, THE LIST IS SO LONG THAT JESUS JUST WANTS ME TO NAME A FEW JOBS.

BULLIES ARE IN EVERY FAMILY, IT'S USUALLY THE LOUD MOUTH COWARD, THAT'S USUALLY LOOKING FOR A HIGH ON SOMETHING.
BULLIES TRIES TO DAMAGE OTHER PEOPLE MENTAL CAPACITY THEY PREY ON THE WEAK, THE ONE THAT RARELY SPEAKS AND THEY LIES UNTIL THEY PASSES OUT ON THEIR OWN LIES, THEN SICKNESS KICKS IN AND DESTROY THEIR FAMILY TREES.

BESIDE EVERY WRONG DOING IS A PENALTY, JESUS IS THE JUDGE AND
JURY, HE'S THE LAWYER THAT NEVER LIES, HE'S THE DOCTOR THAT CURES BEYOND THE BONES, HE KNOWS BULLIES BY NAME, HE'S PROTECTING HIS ANGELS FROM WRONGFUL CONVICTIONS, PERSECUTION AND SHAME, SO JESUS PLANT HIS OFFICE BEHIND EVERY SCENE. IT'S CALLED FREEDOM VALLEY.

4
CHAPTER

◆ ◆ ◆

WELCOME BULLIES WITH OPEN ARMS, LISTEN TO THEM WITHOUT UTTERING A WORD. SMILE IN A MOMENT OF SILENCE, LISTEN TO THEIR
LIES, DON'T BE AFRAID, JESUS IS RIGHT BESIDE YOU, TAKING NOTES,
HE'S INVISIBLE TO THEM, ONLY YOU WILL BE ABLE TO SEE HIM. LET THE BULLY EXHAUST THEMSELVES WITH THEIR LIES. THE COMMON DENOMINATOR GAME HAS NO VALUE IN HEAVEN. PRAY WHEN I COME TO YOUR RESCUE. LOOK, LISTEN, AND FEEL. YOU WERE ONCE AN EMT
IT'S CALL SCENE SAFETY.

BULLIES, WILL BULLY UNTIL THEY'RE OUT OF BULLYING MATERIALS
THEN THEY WILL GEAR UP LIKE A V8 ENGINE THEN TRY TO BLAME EVERYTHING ON YOU. THEY FORGOT THAT CAMERAS ARE EVERYWHERE FOLLOWING YOU. BULLIES MUST TAKE A BACK SEAT FOR A WHILE JUST TO SEE HOW THAT FEELS, THEN MOONWALK INTO THE FUTURE THEN MOVE FORWARD NOT TO TRIP OVER THEMSELVES.

5

CHAPTER

❖ ❖ ❖

PRAYING DAILY IS A MUST. I ASK GOD TO KEEP BULLIES AWAY FROM ME.
I PRAY IN THE CHAPEL BEFORE MY ASSIGNMENT, THEN I
FEEL GOOD ABOUT MYSELF FOR A MOMENT, UNTIL I OPEN THE
DOOR AND WALK INTO A NOISY ENVIRONMENT, ASKING A QUESTION
IS ALMOST IMPOSSIBLE, THEN I GET CALLED IN THE OFFICE, WITH
WHAT OTHERS SAYS, THAT'S IS SAID, THAT WASN'T SAID, THAT I SAID,
I KNOW THAT LINE IS CONFUSING.

THAT'S THE BOILING POINT, THAT'S WHERE INVISIBLE COVID-19 ENTERS THE WORLD TO SEND
A STATEMENT. EVERYONE WILL WEAR A MASK TO PROTECT THEIR CHARACTER. EVERYONE
WILL START FROM GROUND ZERO WITH CORRECT POLICIES AND PROTOCOLS IN PLACE.
SAFETY WILL ALWAYS BE ON THE FRONT BURNER, NO MATTER WHERE IN THE WORLD WE
RESIDE. CODE OF CONDUCT IS NOT ONLY TO BE ON THE WALL, PRACTICE WHAT WE PREACH.

AWAY WITH ALL BULLIES IN THE WORKPLACE AND CHURCHES
EVERYONE IS WELCOME AT JESUS TABLE, EAT AND BE HAPPY.
MONEY HAS NO VALUE IN HEAVEN. ANGELS ARE NOT BULLYING
OTHER ANGELS, EVERYONE IS HAPPY AND PEACEFUL.

IF I SHOULD ASK MY GUARDIAN ANGEL DR MANGUE WHAT TO DO
WITH THE BULLIES WHO SEES ME AS A TARGET, I AM SURE HE WOULD
SAY, DON'T GIVE THEM THE TIME OF THE DAY. AND IF YOU DO, STOP YOUR BREATH FOR AN
INTAKE, THEN DON'T BE AFRAID TO FART ON THE SIDELINE OF THE BULLY. IT WILL NOT SMELL
FOR WHILE.

THIS COULD BE YOUR FIRST TOUCHDOWN IN AMERICA.
FREE YOUR MIND, LIVE YOUR LIFE WITH CONFIDENCE, ASCP CERTIFICATION IS THE HIGHEST IN
THIS FIELD. NO NEED FOR PITY PARTY. WHEN SOMEONE LIE AND TRY TO CALL YOUR NAME, PRAY
FOR THEM. JESUS WILL JUDGE ACCORDINGLY . LET EVERYONE FEND
FOR THEMSELVES.

THE TRUTH WILL PREVAIL.ON EVERY CRISIS CALL.
HURRICANES, STORMS, EARTHQUAKES, ACCIDENTS
ARE ALL EXAMPLES OF GOD'S POWER SPEAKING.
CANCER, HEART DISEASES AND DIABETES ARE A FEW
DIAGNOSIS THAT DOESN'T PLAY GAMES. WORK FOR
JESUS IN 911 EMERGENCY.

LOVE, LOVE, LOVE EVERYBODY, LORD I PRAY THAT AT THIS POINT
MY FART WON'T BE NECESSARY, BECAUSE YOU TAKE CONTROL OF
THE MANY FARTS THAT PLAGUES THE FREEDOM OF YOUR ANGELS.
FORGIVE US ALL, LET'S US NOT BLAME FARTS ON CABBAGE, BROCKLEY OR BEANS ANYMORE,
BUT BY THE WAY WE TREAT OTHERS.

RESPECT EACH OTHER, LOVE EACH OTHER. HATRED AND JEALOUSY
IS A BULLY MENTALITY, THEN THEIR LIES WILL FOLLOW, TO SET THEIR TARGET. JESUS, JESUS,
JESUS PLEASE HEAL US ALL.

AMERICA AND JAMAICA WILL SOMEDAY GET ALONG
THE CRAZY STIMA HAS BEEN GIVEN TO ONE COUNTRY WAY TOO LONG.
AT THIS POINT THE SUN IS ON MY FENCE AND THE RAIN IS STILL MY BLESSING. JESUS FREEDOM
DON'T COST A THING. MONEY HAS NOT VALUE IN HEAVEN.

STOP, STOP, STOP BULLYING IN THE WORKPLACE, OR ELSE I AM GOING TO FART THE FART OF
FREEDOM AGAIN. SORRY BUT I DON'T HAVE TO FIT IN FOR NO REASON THAT WILL SOMEDAY
MAKES SENSE. HMM!!
REGULATE EVERY HEART RHYTHM WITH OUR LOYAL FRIENDS, DOGS CATS AND RABBITS TOO.
OH THIS IS LOVE, BRING IN JESUS DOVES.
SHALOM.

6

CHAPTER

❖◆❖◆❖

THE WORLD IS COMING TO AN END
FIGHTING AND PLOTTING TO TARNISH
ONES CHARACTER WILL NOT WORK
ANYMORE, JESUS HAS FULL CONTROL
IN EVERY SITUATION, HE'S THE GREATEST.
COVID-19 HAS DRAWN PEOPLE TOGETHER
WHO WOULD NORMALLY BE APART.
BULLIES ARE STILL ON THE SIDELINE
WAITING FOR A TOUCHDOWN.
BUT THEY WILL BE WAITING IN VAIN.

THERE'S MORE THAN ENOUGH WORK
TO KEEP EVERYONE ON THEIR FEET.
WORKPLACE SHOULD BE A SAFE HAVEN
FOR ALL. SO WHEN I NEED A PRAYER THE
CHAPEL CALLS MY NAME, BEFORE I FALL.
HEALING IS COMING IN THE MOMENT WE
LEAST EXPECTED. NEW FRIENDS NEW
BEGINNINGS ARE AROUND THE BEND.
BULLYING WILL BE A THING IN THE PAST
SO IS RACISM, BUT ONLY TIME WILL TELL.
FREE EVERY MINDS FROM GOING TO HELL
FORGIVE, BUT NOT EVERYONE WILL HAVE
ALZHEIMER'S TO FORGET THEIR EXPERIENCES.
WE WILL MOVE ON TO GROW WITH OUR FAITH
IN HAND. FART IS NOT A DISEASE, ITS HOT AIR
WITH A SMELL OF WHATEVER FOOD WE CONSUMED
AND DIGESTED AND WILLING TO SHARE. THIS
ANGLE WILL NOT PUT YOU IN JAIL. SO STAY
FOCUS AND BE AWARE. OF YOUR SURROUNDINGS.
NOW ALL CLEAR.

7

CHAPTER

❖❖❖❖

THIS'S THE CHAPTER WHEN JESUS PUT A SMILE ON MY FACE, ITS APRIL 7TH AND ITS MY BIRTHDAY 🎂 NO FARTING AROUND MY CAKE PLEASE. IN THIS ROOM THERE WILL BE NO BULLYING. SO LET YOUR WIGS DOWN AND START DANCING. TAKE ALL MASK OFF AND START LAUGHING 😄 IT'S ALL CLEAR THAT WE HAVE OUR VACCINES 💉. THIS PARTY IS A BOOSTER, iT'S A SEVEN LINER FOR ALL TIMERS. LET LOOSE, BE A GOOSEY GOOSE. FUNNY FUN MI A GLASS OF JUICE. COME BACK TO EARTH AND FACE REALITY.

SORRY THIS WORLD IS A WICKED PLACE
KEEP YOUR CIRCLE SMALL, CHERISH TRUE FRIENDSHIPS. TRUST AND LET TRUST, TRUST THE TRUST THAT GOD TRUSTED IN YOU. GIVE THE GIFT OF FREEDOM CAPTION THE HEART THATS MADE OF GOLD. FAITH, FAMILY AND A FEWS FRINDS WILL HAVE AND TO HOLD.
STAYING HUMBLE AND TRUE TO YOURSELF FIRST. FORGIVE THE ENEMY ITS CALL COVID-19 IT'S THE BULLY IN THE NATION.

USE YOUR GIFT VERY WISELY, PRAYER IS THE NUMBER ONE 💊 MEDICINE, DR MANGUE IS STILL A MENTOR IN HEAVEN HE'S A FOREVER GUARDIAN ANGEL.
FART ON THE BULLY BOOK 14th. EvERY
GIFTED CHILD NEEDS FREEDOM TO FEEL FREE. A FRESH START TO BE THEMSELVES.

BULLYING IS WRONG, STOP MY POEMS
ARE TALKING TO THE WORLD.
Stop!
Stop!
Stop the Bullying 'STAT'.
Never used it PRN.
Bullying is a SIN.
It works from Within.
Stop! All Bullying.
Please!!.

FINAL CHAPTER ON
THIS JOURNEY.

Policemen are Bullies too, they uses their power to abuse the System. They Target
Innocent people, just to prove a point.▱
Then they wonder why so many things are going wrong in their personal lives .
Judges are Bullies too, the justice System is a Rig A buff Buff. Jesus Money is moving around to purchase
big Mansions and Luxury Cars from Mars and Jupiter with Rockets 🚀
Yacht and houses in Grand Cayman Island.
How do I know all this, it's because I FART ON ALL BULLIES on the Sideline for Facts.

Forgive us all, dearest Jesus, Blood Pressures are sky high. Temperatures are to the Roof. Rebuild our
differences, let us agree to disagree. So that the next Group will smile and Say. BE A BUDDY, NOT A
BULLY.
Let's 🕋 Pray that the Future will be much greater than today.
I Am an AUTHOR ✍

UNIVERSAL JOKE

WHY DID THE GIFTED BOY
AND GIFTED GIRL, ATE
THEIR HOMEWORK TOGETHER?

Answer: BECAUSE THE TEACHER
TOLD THE CLASS, THAT IT WAS
A PIECE OF CHEESE CAKE.

Smile, it's okay to Smile.
To every Gifted Child.
Fart on the Bully.

POETRY

YOU TRIED TO TARNISH
OUR CHARACTER,
BUT YOU COULD'NT
TOUCH OUR REPUTATION.
WHEN YOU'RE LOOKING
FOR THE WEAKEST LINK
REMEMBER JESUS HAS THE
STRONGEST WAITING TO
THINK . JUST TO UNDERSTAND
THIS FULLY, EVERY GIFTED CHILD
SHOULD FART ON THE BULLY.
TEACH THEM A LESSON FROM THE
BOOK OF KARMA. DON'T GET DIZZY
ON THE GROUND. WHAT GOES UP
WILL COME DOWN. SAFETY FIRST
IS WHY WE TOOK THIS RHOUTE .
NOT EVEN THE STOP SIGN DIDN'T
WORK. SO WE MAKE A U-TURN AND
FART ON THE BULLY. TO EVERY BULLY
IN THE WORLD. BE A BUDDY, NOT A
BULLY. PASS THIS TEST, WITH FLYING
COLOR. YAY!! We're BULLY FREE.

MY MOTTO TO LIVE
BY IN AMERICA.

❖◆❖◆❖

I DON'T WANT ANY FAKE FRIENDS
AND I REALLY DON'T WANT ANY
REAL ENEMIES.
BLESSINGS.
Amen 🕌

FINAL CHAPTER ON THIS JOURNEY.

Policemen are Bullies too, they uses their power to abuse the System.
They Target Innocent people, just to prove a point.▭
Then they wonder why so many things are going wrong in their personal lives.
Judges are Bullies too, the justice System is a Rig A buff Buff.
Jesus Money is moving around to purchase big Mansions and
Luxury Cars from Mars and Jupiter with Rockets 🚀
Yacht and houses in Grand Cayman Island.
How do I know all this, it's because I FART ON ALL BULLIES
on the Sideline for Facts.

Forgive us all, dearest Jesus, Blood Pressures are sky high.
Temperatures are to the Roof. Rebuild our differences,
let us agree to disagree. So that the next Group will smile and Say.
BE A BUDDY, NOT A BULLY.
Let's 🛐 Pray that the Future will be much greater than today.
I Am an AUTHOR ✍

SHALOM, PEACE FOR EVERY FAMILY IN THE WORLD. LOVE EACH OTHER, PROTECT THE GIFTED ONES IN JESUS NAME. LISEN TO THE DOVES.